the knit}
generation}

15 Great Patterns by 8 Hot Designers

Sarah Hatton

STACKPOLE BOOKS

Guilford, Connecticut

Published by Stackpole Books
An imprint of Globe Pequot
www.rowman.com

Distributed by
NATIONAL BOOK NETWORK
800-462-6420

Copyright © 2014 by Quail Publishing
First Stackpole Books paperback edition, 2017

This edition of *The Knit Generation* first
published in the UK by Quail Publishing in 2014 is published by
arrangement with Silke Bruenink Agency, Munich, Germany.

Designs: Andi Satterlund, Anni Howard, Gemma Atkinson, Ivar Asplund,
Karie Westermann, Rachel Atkinson, Rachel Coopey, Sara Thornett

Pattern Checking: Jill Gray
Photography: India Hobson
Technique Photography: Quail Publishing
Styling: Sarah Hatton
Graphic Design: Darren Brant

British Library Cataloguing in Publication Information Available

Library of Congress Cataloging-in-Publication Data Available

ISBN 978-0-8117-1785-4 (pbk.)

♾™ The paper used in this publication meets the minimum requirements
of American National Standard for Information Sciences—Permanence of
Paper for Printed Library Materials, ANSI/NISO Z39.48-1992.

Printed in the United Kingdom

The Knit Generation designers

Andi Satterlund started knitting to keep her hands busy while indulging in her love for movies. She began designing for fun while in college, and the stunning costumes of her favorite old movies provided her with inspiration. Andi now writes knitting patterns for a living from her home in Seattle, WA, USA. When she's not knitting, Andi spends her time writing on her blog, watching movies, and drinking too much tea.
Find out more about Andi at – www.untangling-knots.com

Anni Howard has worked in the UK knit design industry for many years, both in-house for a yarn spinning company and as an independent freelance designer. She loves integrating different textures into a garment, mixing up colours and yarns, and working out interesting shapes and constructions. Her pattern in this book uses a traditional technique and modern chunky Rowan yarns in rich shades to create easy and quick-to-knit mitts, ensuring toasty warm hands even in the depths of winter. Find Anni's work at http://www.ravelry.com/designers/anni-howard. Read her blog at http://annidomino.blogspot.co.uk/

Gemma Atkinson. I was born in County Durham and grew up in a small seaside town, always wanting to paint or draw or do something creative. I studied A levels at college in Textiles, Psychology and English Language before going on to study Textile Design at the University of Huddersfield specialising in printed textiles. Always having had a love of colour and texture, I worked on creating trend lead fabrics (both digitally printed and screen printed) for fashion and home interiors. After graduating with a Bachelor of Arts degree I stayed and worked temporarily in a bar until I could find the perfect job, still keeping myself heavily involved in crafts of all kinds to keep my creativity flowing. I was offered an assistant designer job for Rowan in 2011, and it was so exciting to be able to get back into designing and to work for such a prestigious hand knit brand. I used my print skills to inspire me to create garments with different stitch textures, colour and pattern placement in simple, wearable shapes.

Ivar Asplund. Born in Västervik, Sweden, in 1973. I live in Stockholm.
My grandmother showed me how to knit when I was perhaps five years old. Some thirty-five years later it keeps getting more and more enjoyable. The more I knit, learn and develop my skills, the more fun it gets! Sweaters and shawls are my favourite things to knit, and I like working with different techniques like stranded colourwork, cables, lace, brioche and twined knitting. It's amazing what you can make with such simple tools.
Find out more about Ivar at – www.asplundknits.blogspot.com

Karie Westermann is originally from Denmark, but lives and works in Glasgow, Scotland. Past collaborators include Rowan Yarns, Baa Ram Ewe and multiple knitting magazines. As a designer, Karie believes in a strong, modern aesthetic that draws upon her Nordic roots and sensibility.
Find out more about Karie at www.fourth-edition.co.uk

Rachel Atkinson. The daughter of a shepherd, wool is literally in Rachel's blood. A full-time career as a knit, crochet and craft Technical Editor and Designer for a host of international magazines, publishers and designers ensures she continues the family tradition of being surrounded by yarn.
Find out more about Rachel at – www.mylifeinknitwear.com

Rachel Coopey. I was taught to knit by my grandmother and mother and I've still got the extremely long garter stitch scarf to prove it! I was drawn to sock knitting by sock yarn. I bought three skeins of hand-dyed sock yarn because they were so beautiful and thought I'd give knitting a pair of socks a try. When I turned the heel on that first sock I felt like I'd performed a magic trick. I pulled it out of my knitting bag and showed it to everyone I came across, shouting 'Look, look what I made! It's a SOCK!' (I got varying degrees of enthusiasm in return, but I think it's fair to say no one was as excited as me). I haven't stopped knitting and designing socks since then. I love the portability of socks, the intricacy and the usefulness of the finished project - there's nothing like hand knitted socks for keeping your feet warm.

Sara Thornett. I enjoy working interesting stitch patterns – patterns that are fluid and easy to construct. When I design, I look to these kinds of patterns as a starting point with the aim to give the knitter an enjoyable experience, as well as an appealing knitted project. Find out more about Sara at – www.sarathornett.com

ROBIN
page 20

FOXGLOVE
page 94

BUD
page 82

ACORN
page 26

HAWTHORN
page 76

HOUNDSTOOTH
page 90

JUNIPER
page 32

LEIGH
page 86

MOUSEAR
page 50

MULCH
page 62

TULLOCH
page 56

YEW
page 72

PINECONES
page 42

ROBIN

rowan felted tweed

BY IVAR ASPLUND

ROBIN

BY IVAR ASPLUND

YARN

Rowan Felted Tweed one ball each of

A - Treacle 145 1 x 50gm

B - Tawny 186 1 x 50gm

Please check your tension carefully as almost a full ball of each shade was used

NEEDLES

3mm (no 11) (US 2/3) circular needles 40cm/16in and 80cm/32in long

Stitch holder

FINISHED SIZE

(Once blocked and when laid flat)

Height (approx.): 28cm/11in

Top width: 24cm/9½in

Bottom width: 50cm/19½in

TENSION

17 sts and 33 rounds to 10cm/4in measured over brioche knitting using 3mm (US 2/3) needles.

Brioche knitting in the round

Brioche knitting is basically K1, P1, but with slipped stitches and yarnovers.

To knit brioche in the round you knit K stitches and slip P stitches on every other row and on the other rows you will slip K stitches and purl P stitches.

Stitches are always slipped purlwise, and before slipping a stitch you bring the yarn to the front to get a yarnover that lies over the slipped stitch. Therefore, yarnovers are not between stitches (the way they are in lace knitting) but over slipped stitches.

Yarnovers are knitted (or purled) tog with the st they lie over.

SPECIAL ABBREVIATIONS

BRK (brioche knit): K the st that was slipped in the previous round tog with its yo.

BRP (brioche purl): P the st that was slipped in the previous round tog with its yo.

sl1pwyif: slip 1 purlwise with yarn in front

On odd-numbered rounds: BRK1 and sl 1 purlwise with yarn in front. (Before slipping a st you bring the yarn to the front and make a yo together with the st as you slip it.) The yo lies over the sl st.

On even-numbered rounds: Sl every K st purlwise (with yarn in front to make a yo at the same time) and BRP every P st.

dec 4: sl 2 sts separately as if to K, transfer them back to left needle and K tog tbl; place next stitch on st holder in front of work; K2 tog; pass the second st on right needle over the first one; transfer the st on holder to left needle, then transfer the first st on right needle to left needle; pass the st which was on the holder over the st to the right of it. Place this st on right needle and sl1pwyif. (4 sts dec and the centre stitch is on top)

inc 4: Into the same st K1, yo, K1, yo, K1; sl next st purlwise with yarn in front.

COWL
Using yarn A and the long-tail method, cast on 252 sts loosely, preferably cast on over 2 needles held together.

Turn work ready to work set up row.
Set up row (RS): Using yarn A, * sl1pwyif, p2tog, rep from * to end. 168 sts.
DO NOT turn work but slide sts to other tip of needle.

Next row: Using yarn B, knit.

All even-numbered rounds are worked with yarn A.

All odd-numbered rounds are worked with yarn B.

Cont as folls:-

Round 1: Using yarn B, * BRK1, sl1pwyif , rep from * to end.

Join to work in round, taking care to ensure sts are not twisted.

Place marker at beg of round.

Round 2: Using yarn A, * sl1pwyif, BRP1, rep from * to end.

Rep rounds 1 and 2 9 times more. (20 rounds worked)

Round 21 (dec row): Using B, (BRK1, sl1pwyif) 6 times, dec 4, (BRK1, sl1pwyif) 11 times, dec 4, (BRK1, sl1pwyif) 11 times, dec 4, (BRK1, sl1pwyif) 11 times, dec 4, (BRK1, sl1pwyif) 11 times, dec 4, (BRK1, sl1pwyif) 5 times. 144 sts.

Round 22: Work as given for round 2.

Rep rounds 1 and 2 9 times. (40 rounds worked).

Round 41(dec round): Using B, (BRK1, sl1pwyif) 5 times, dec 4, (BRK1, sl1pwyif) 9 times, dec 4, (BRK1, sl1pwyif) 9 times, dec 4, (BRK1, sl1pwyif) 9 times, dec 4, (BRK1, sl1pwyif) 9 times, dec 4, (BRK1, sl1pwyif) 4 times. 120 sts.

Round 42: Work as given for round 2.

Rep rounds 1 and 2 9 times. (60 rounds worked).

Round 61 (dec round): Using B, (BRK1, sl1pwyif) 4 times, dec 4, (BRK1, sl1pwyif) 7 times, dec 4, (BRK1, sl1pwyif) 7 times, dec 4, (BRK1 sl1pwyif) 7 times, dec 4, (BRK1, sl1pwyif) 7 times, dec 4, (BRK1, sl1pwyif) 7 times, dec 4, (BRK1 sl1pwyif) 3 times. 96 sts.

Round 62: Work as given for round 2.

Rep rounds 1 and 2 9 times. (80 rounds worked).

Round 81 (inc and dec round): Using B, ***** inc 4, (BRK1, sl1pwyif) twice, dec 4, (BRK1, sl1pwyif) twice, rep from * to end. 96 sts (24 sts dec and 24 sts inc)

Round 82: Work as given for round 2 (except that you will purl into the yos of each inc 4).

Rep rounds 1 and 2 9 times. (100 rounds worked).

Round 101 (inc and dec round): Work as given for round 81 but starting and ending the round with (BRK1, sl1pwyif).

Round 102: Work as given for round 82.

Rep rounds 1 and 2 9 times. (120 rounds worked).

Round 121 (inc and dec round): Work as given for round 81 but starting the round with (BRK1, sl1pwyif) twice and ending the round with dec 4 and sl1pwyif.

Round 122: Work as given for round 2 (except that you purl the inc yos)

Work as given for rounds 1 and 2 once more.

Cast off loosely with B.

FINISHING
Sew in ends but do not trim. Pin cowl out to dimensions given, cover with damp cloths and leave until dry. When shawl has dried, trim ends.

ACORN

rowan pure wool worsted

BY RACHEL ATKINSON

ACORN

BY RACHEL ATKINSON

SIZE

38cm (15in) wide x 218cm (86in) long

YARN

Rowan Pure Wool Worsted

3 balls x 100gm

(shown in Gold 133)

NEEDLES & ACCESSORIES

1 pair of 5mm (no 6)(US 8) knitting needles

Cable needle

TENSION

Each 51 sts and 24 rows of 1 chart rep measures 40cm (15½in) wide x 12cm (4¾in) long after blocking.

SPECIAL ABBREVIATIONS

C5F   **Cable 5 Front:** Slip 2 sts to cable needle and hold at front, k3, k2 from cable needle.

C5B   **Cable 5 Back:** Slip 3 sts to cable needle and hold at back, k2, k3 from cable needle.

MB   **Make Bobble:** Into 1 stitch work (k1, yo, k1, yo, k1), turn, p5, turn, k5, turn, p2tog, p1, p2tog, turn, sk2po.

PATTERN NOTES

The length is easy to adjust to suit. Simply work less or more repeats of the chart and finish as instructed.

CHART-WRITTEN INSTRUCTIONS

Row 1 (RS): K2, MB, k8, k2tog, yo, k1, yo, ssk, k1, k2tog, yo, k1, yo, ssk, k3, MB, k3, k2tog, yo, k1, yo, ssk, k1, k2tog, yo, k1, yo, ssk, k8, MB, k2.

Row 2 (WS): P5, k6, p29, k6, p5.

Row 3: K10, k2tog, yo, k3, yo, sk2po, yo, k3, yo, ssk, k5, k2tog, yo, k3, yo, sk2po, yo, k3, yo, ssk, k10.

Row 4: P5, k4, p33, k4, p5.

Row 5: K8, [k2tog, yo, k1, yo, ssk, k1] 5 times, k2tog, yo, k1, yo, ssk, k8.

Row 6: P5, k3, p35, k3, p5.

Row 7: C5F, k2, k2tog, [yo, k3, yo, sk2po] 5 times, yo, k3, yo, ssk, k2, C5B.

Row 8: P5, k2, p37, k2, p5.

Row 9: K8, yo, ssk, k1, k2tog, yo, k7, [yo, ssk, k1, k2tog, yo, k1] twice, k6, yo, ssk, k1, k2tog, yo, k8.

Row 10: P5, k3, p35, k3, p5.

Row 11: [K9, yo, sk2po, yo] twice, k3, [yo, sk2po, yo, k9] twice.

Row 12: P5, k4, p33, k4, p5.

Row 13: K8, k2tog, yo, k1, yo, ssk, k3, MB, k3, k2tog, yo, k1, yo, ssk, k1, k2tog, yo, k1, yo, ssk, k3, MB, k3, k2tog, yo, k1, yo, ssk, k8.

Row 14: P5, k3, p35, k3, p5.

Row 15: K7, k2tog, yo, k3, yo, ssk, k5, k2tog, yo, k3, yo, sk2po, yo, k3, yo, ssk, k5, k2tog, yo, k3, yo, ssk, k7.

Row 16: P5, k2, p37, k2, p5.

Row 17: K8, [yo, ssk, k1, k2tog, yo, k1] 6 times, k7.

Row 18: P5, k3, p35, k3, p5.

Row 19: C5F, k4, [yo, sk2po, yo, k3] 6 times, k1, C5B.

Row 20: P5, k4, p33, k4, p5.

Row 21: K11, yo, ssk, k1, k2tog, yo, k1, yo, ssk, k1, k2tog, yo, k7, yo, ssk, k1, k2tog, yo, k1, yo, ssk, k1, k2tog, yo, k11.

Row 22: P5, k6, p29, k6, p5.

Row 23: K12, yo, sk2po, yo, k3, yo, sk2po, yo, k9, yo, sk2po, yo, k3, yo, sk2po, yo, k12.

Row 24: P5, k7, p27, k7, p5.

SCARF

Using the long tail method, loosely cast on 51 sts.

Knit 1 row.

Rows 1 to 24 of chart set pattern.

Rep these 24 rows 18 times, or until work reaches desired length.

Work row 1 only once more.

Knit 2 rows.

Cast off loosely knitwise on **WS**.

FINISHING

Weave in all ends. Block to measurements taking care to pin out the central point between the cable crosses. Leave to dry thoroughly before unpinning and trimming ends.

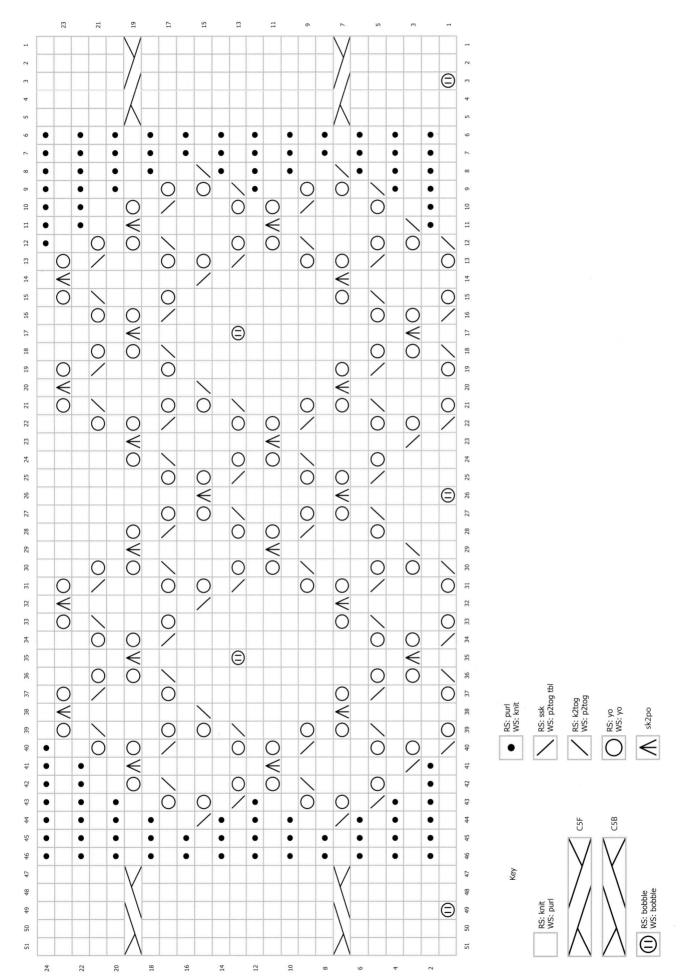

Key

RS: knit
WS: purl

RS: bobble
WS: bobble

C5F

C5B

RS: purl
WS: knit

RS: ssk
WS: p2tog tbl

RS: k2tog
WS: p2tog

RS: yo
WS: yo

sk2po

JUNIPER

rowan felted tweed & kidsilk haze

BY KARIE WESTERMANN

JUNIPER

BY KARIE WESTERMANN

YARN

Rowan Felted Tweed DK

A – Clay 177   1 x 50gm

Rowan Kidsilk Haze

B – Cream 634 1 x 25gm

NEEDLES

3.25mm (no 10) (US 3) circular needle, 40cm/16in long

4mm (no 8) (US 6) circular needle, 40cm/16in long

TENSION

18 sts and 24 rounds to 10cm/4in measured over pattern using 4mm (US 6) needles and ONE END OF EACH YARN HELD TOGETHER.

FINISHED SIZE

To fit an average sized adult head

Approx. 56cm/22in in circumference

Note: Watch your tension as the hat uses almost exactly one ball of Rowan Felted Tweed DK. If you are a loose knitter, you may require a second ball.

HAT

Using 3.25mm (US 3) needles and 1 strand of each yarn HELD TOGETHER, cast on 96 sts.

Join to work in round, taking care to ensure sts are not twisted.

Place marker at beg of round.

Round 1: * K1, p1, rep from * to end.

Rep this round 9 times more.

Change to 4mm (US 6) needles.

Next round: K1, * m1, k2, rep from * to last st, m1, k1. 144 sts.

Cont as folls:-

Round 1: K to end.

Round 2: * P2, k4, rep from * to end.

Round 3: K to end.

Round 4: * K3, p2, k1, rep from * to end.

These 4 rounds set pattern.

Cont in patt as set until work measures 12cm/4½in from top of rib.

Shape crown

Round 1: K to end.

Round 2: P to end.

Round 3: K2, * k2tog, k4, rep from * to last 4 sts, k2tog, k2. 120 sts.

Round 4: P to end.

Round 5: K to end.

Round 6: P to end.

Round 7: K2, * k2tog, k3, rep from * to last 3 sts, k2tog, k1. 96 sts.

Round 8: P to end.

Round 9: K to end.

Round 10: P to end.

Round 11: K1, * k2tog, k2, rep from * to last 3 sts, k2tog, k1. 72 sts.

Round 12: P to end.

Round 13: K to end.

Round 14: P to end.

Round 15: K1, * k2tog, k1, rep from * to last 2 sts, k2tog. 48 sts.

Round 16: P to end.

Round 17: K to end.

Round 18: P to end.

Round 19: K2tog to end. 24 sts.

Round 20: P to end.

Round 21: K2tog to end. 12 sts.

Break yarn and thread through rem sts.

Fasten off.

FINISHING

Weave in ends but do not trim. Make pompon approx. 6cm/2½in in diameter, using leftover yarn. Block hat to size and secure pompon on top of crown. Trim ends.

KIMBER

rowan pure wool 4 ply

BY RACHEL COOPEY

KIMBER

BY RACHEL COOPEY

YARN

Rowan Pure Wool 4 ply

2 x 50gm

(shown in Claret 466)

NEEDLES

3.25mm (no 10) (US 3) 40cm/16in circular needle

or dpns

3.5mm (no 9/10) (US 4) 40cm/16in circular needle

or dpns

Cable needle

FINISHED SIZE

Circumference- 75cm/29½in, intended to be worn
with 15-20.5cm/6-8in positive ease.

TENSION

26 sts and 36 rounds to 10cm/4in measured over cable
chart using 3.5mm (US 4) needles.

SPECIAL ABBREVIATIONS

2/1 RC: Slip next 2 sts to cable needle and place at front
of work, k1, then k2 from cable needle.

2/1 LC: Slip next st to cable needle and place at back of
work, k2, then k1 from cable needle.

2/1 RPC: Slip next st to cable needle and place at back of
work, k2, then p1 from cable needle.

2/1 LPC: Slip next 2 sts to cable needle and place at front
of work, p1, then k2 from cable needle.

2/2 RC: Slip next 2 sts to cable needle and place at back
of work, k2, then k2 from cable needle.

2/2 LC: Slip next 2 sts to cable needle and place at front
of work, k2, then k2 from cable needle.

Central double decrease: slip 2 sts as if to k2tog, k1,
pass the 2 slipped sts over.

M1L: Make 1 Left: Insert left needle, from front to back,
under strand of yarn which runs between next stitch on
left needle and last stitch on right needle; knit this stitch
through back loop. 1 stitch increased.

M1R: Make 1 Right: Insert left needle, from back to front, under strand of yarn which runs between next stitch on left needle and last stitch on right needle; knit this stitch through front loop. 1 stitch increased.

HAT

Using 3.25mm (US 3) needle, cast on 165 sts.

Join to work in round, taking care to ensure sts are not twisted. Place marker at beg of round.

Work rounds 1-5 of chart A 3 times, then work rounds 1-3 once more. The chart is worked 5 times across the round. 18 rounds.

Change to 3.5mm (US 4) needle.

Inc Round: * P1, k1, M1R, k1, M1L, k1, p2, k4, p1, rep from * to end of round. 195 sts.

Work rounds 1-30 of chart B once then work rounds 1-16 once more. The chart is worked 5 times across the round. 46 rounds.

Work rounds 1-22 of chart C, changing to dpns when needed. The chart is worked 5 times across the round. 45 sts rem.

Round 1: Knit.

Round 2: *K2tog, rep from * to last st, k1. 23 sts.

Round 3: Knit.

Round 4: *K2tog, rep from * to last st, k1. 12 sts.

FINISHING

Cut yarn, leaving a 15cm/6in tail, draw the tail through the remaining stitches and fasten off. Weave in ends and block.

Chart A

33	32	31	30	29	28	27	26	25	24	23	22	21	20	19	18	17	16	15	14	13	12	11	10	9	8	7	6	5	4	3	2	1	
•					•	•				•	•	╲╱		╲		•	•				•	•					•	•				•	5
•					•	•				•	•					•	•				•	•					•	•				•	4
•					•	•				•	•					•	•				•	•					•	•				•	3
•					•	•				•	•					•	•				•	•					•	•				•	2
•					•	•				•	•					•	•				•	•					•	•				•	1

| 33 | 32 | 31 | 30 | 29 | 28 | 27 | 26 | 25 | 24 | 23 | 22 | 21 | 20 | 19 | 18 | 17 | 16 | 15 | 14 | 13 | 12 | 11 | 10 | 9 | 8 | 7 | 6 | 5 | 4 | 3 | 2 | 1 |

Chart B

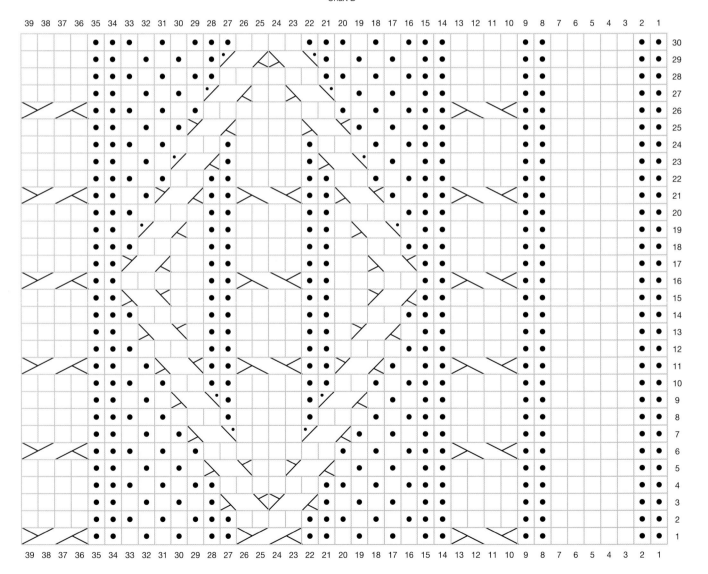

Chart C

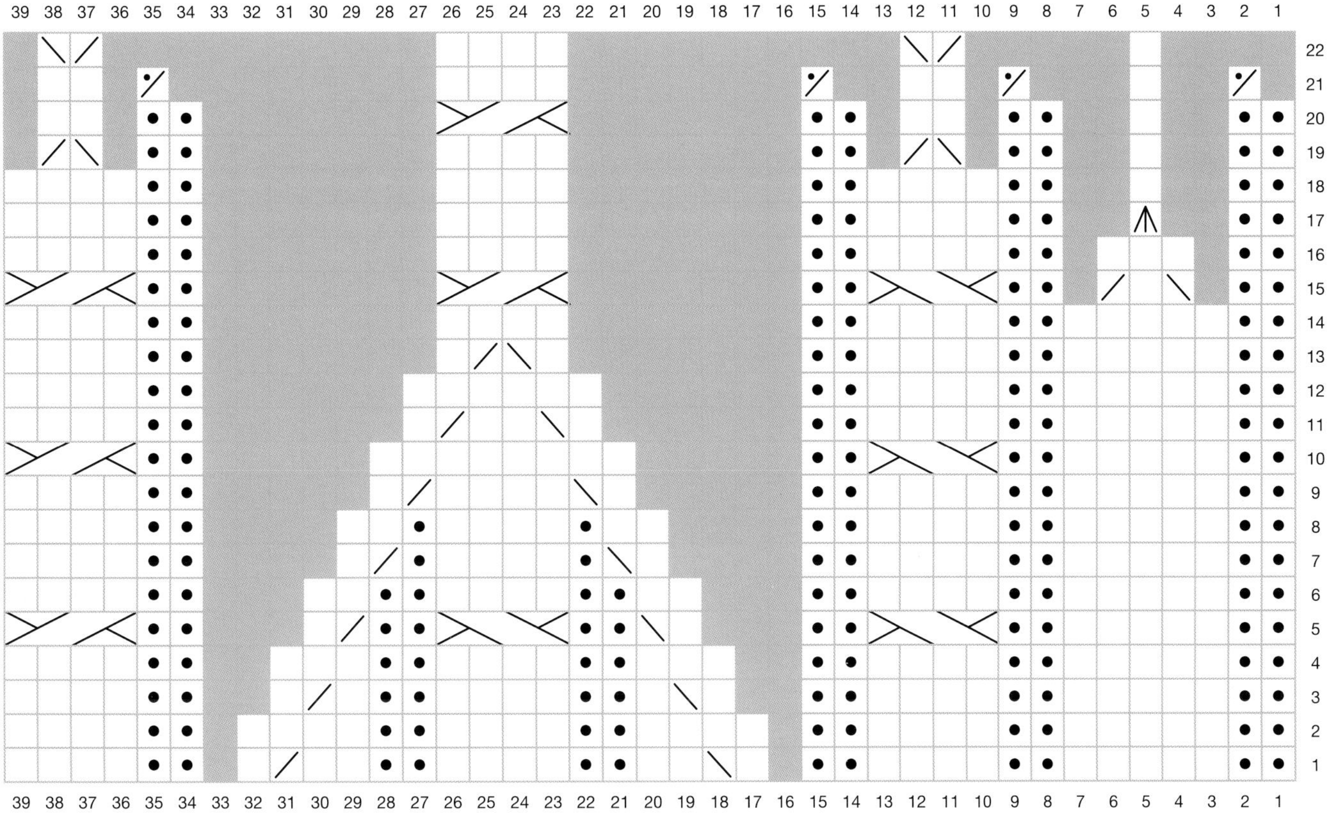

39 38 37 36 35 34 33 32 31 30 29 28 27 26 25 24 23 22 21 20 19 18 17 16 15 14 13 12 11 10 9 8 7 6 5 4 3 2 1

22
21
20
19
18
17
16
15
14
13
12
11
10
9
8
7
6
5
4
3
2
1

39 38 37 36 35 34 33 32 31 30 29 28 27 26 25 24 23 22 21 20 19 18 17 16 15 14 13 12 11 10 9 8 7 6 5 4 3 2 1

Key

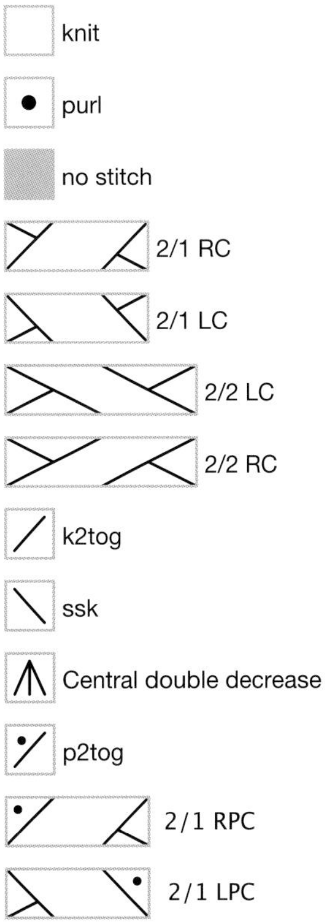

knit	
•	purl
	no stitch
	2/1 RC
	2/1 LC
	2/2 LC
	2/2 RC
╱	k2tog
╲	ssk
⋀	Central double decrease
• ╱	p2tog
	2/1 RPC
	2/1 LPC

PINECONES

rowan fine art

BY KARIE WESTERMANN

PINECONES

BY KARIE WESTERMANN

TENSION

17 sts and 30 rows to 10cm/4in measured over st st on 4mm (US 6) needles.

PATTERN NOTES

On all charts only RS rows are shown, WS rows should be worked: K2, purl to last 2 sts, k2.

The charts show the left-hand side of the shawl. After you have knitted the centre stitch work the lace chart again from left to right omitting the edge sts. As the shawl is symmetrical, this will mirror the stitch pattern around the centre st.

Remember to slip markers at edge stitches and around centre stitch throughout.

If you wish to create a larger shawl, begin working charts once there are 191 sts. Please note you will require a second skein of yarn for the larger size.

SHAWL

Cast on 2 sts.

Knit 10 rows.

Row 11: K2, turn work 90 degrees, pick up and knit 1 stitch from each of the 3 g st ridges along the side edge, then pick up 2 stitches from your cast-on edge. 7 sts.

Row 12 (WS): K2, p3, k2.

Row 13: K2, pm, yo, k1, yo, pm, k1, pm, yo, k1, yo, pm, k2. 11 sts.

Row 14: K2, purl to last 2 sts, k2.

Row 15: K2, sm, yo, knit to centre stitch, yo, sm, k1, sm, yo, knit to last 2 sts, yo, sm, k2. 15 sts.

Row 16 and every foll alt row: K2, purl to last 2 sts, k2.

Rep last 2 rows 34 times more. 151 sts.

Work as set on Chart A once. 207 sts.

Work as set on Chart B once. 263 sts.

Work as set on Chart C once. 299 sts.

Work WS row as set.

Cast off using a stretchy cast-off: K2, * put both sts back onto left needle, k2tog tbl, k1, rep from * to end.

FINISHING

Soak the shawl in lukewarm water and squeeze out excess water without wringing. Weave in ends, but do not cut. Pin shawl out to desired dimensions. When shawl has dried, trim ends.

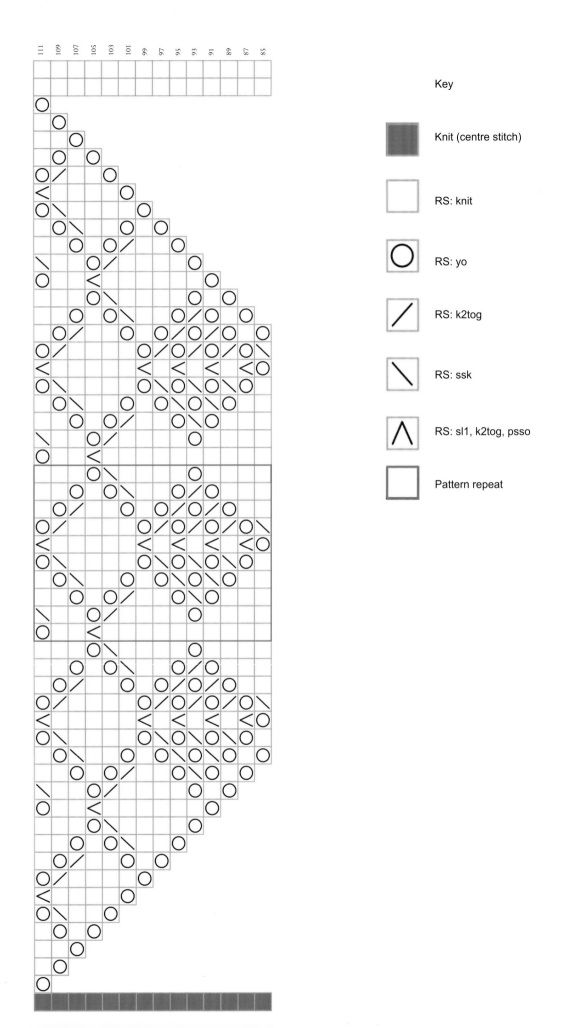

Chart A

Key

Knit (centre stitch)

RS: knit

RS: yo

RS: k2tog

RS: ssk

RS: sl1, k2tog, psso

Pattern repeat

Chart B

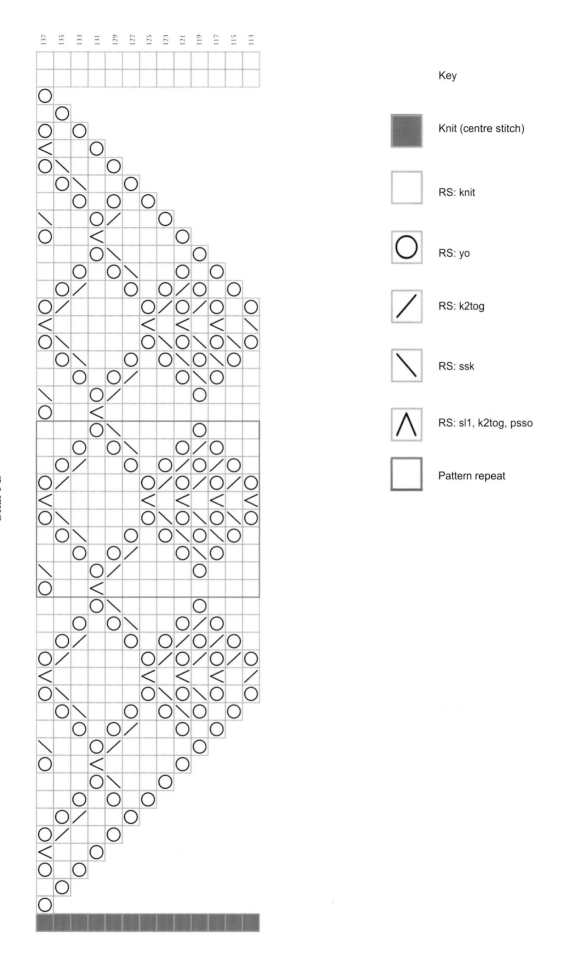

Key

Knit (centre stitch)

RS: knit

RS: yo

RS: k2tog

RS: ssk

RS: sl1, k2tog, psso

Pattern repeat

Chart C

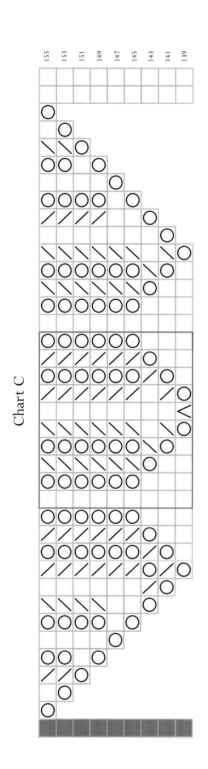

	Knit (centre stitch)
	RS: knit
○	RS: yo
/	RS: k2tog
\	RS: ssk
∧	RS: sl1, k2tog, psso
	Pattern repeat

MOUSEAR

rowan cocoon & tumble

BY ANNI HOWARD

MOUSEAR

BY ANNI HOWARD

SIZES

S/M [M/L]

Actual size around palm (mitt is approx. 3cm/1in larger to allow for thumbs) 23 [25.5] cm/9 [10] in

YARN

Rowan Cocoon

A – Quarry Tile 818 1 [2] x 100gm balls

Rowan Tumble

B – Amethyst 568   1 [1] x 100gm ball

NEEDLES

Set of four double-pointed 6.5mm (no 3) (US 10) needles or circular needle if using the magic loop technique

Set of four double-pointed 7mm (no 2) (US 10½) needles or circular needle if using the magic loop technique

Stitch holder

TENSION

14 sts and 18 rounds to 10cm/4in measured over thrummed patt using 7mm (US 10½) needles.

BEFORE YOU START

Cut thrums – you will need approx. 130 - 150 thrums per mitt. Use B and cut each thrum approx. 15cm/6in long.

SPECIAL ABBREVIATION

T1 = thrum one stitch, K next stitch using A and short length of B together.

Left mitt

Using 6.5mm needles (US 10) and B, cast on 24 [27] sts and join to work in the round.

Purl 2 rounds.

Break off B and join in A.

Inc round: (K3, m1 [by picking up loop between last and next st and working into the back of this loop]) 8 [9] times. 32 [36] sts.

Round 1: *K2, p2, rep from * to end.

Work this round 11 times more.

Change to 7mm (US 10½) needles and knit 2 rounds.

Cont as folls:-

Round 1: *K3, T1, rep from * to end.

Round 2: Knit to end, ensuring you knit together both strands of thrummed sts.

Round 3: *K1, T1, k2, rep from * to end.

Round 4: As round 2.

Shape thumb

Round 1: *K3, T1, rep from * to last 4 sts, m1, k3, m1, T1. 34 [38] sts.

Round 2: Knit to end, ensuring you knit together both strands of thrummed sts.

Round 3: *K1, T1, k2, rep from * to last 6 sts, m1, k2, T1, k2, m1, k1. 36 [40] sts.

Round 4: As round 2.

Round 5: *K3, T1, rep from * to last 8 sts, m1, k1, T1, k3, T1, k1, m1, T1. 38 [42] sts.

Round 6: As round 2.

Round 7: *K1, T1, k2, rep from * to last 10 sts, m1, T1, (k3, T1) twice, m1, k1. 40 [44] sts.

Round 8: As round 2.

Round 9: *K3, T1, rep from * to last 12 sts, m1, [k3, T1] twice, k3, m1, T1. 42 [46] sts.

Round 10: As round 2.

Round 11: *K1, T1, k2, rep from * to last 14 sts, m1, k2, T1, (k3, T1) twice, k2, m1, k1. 44 [48] sts.

Round 12: As round 2.

Divide for thumb

Next round: Patt 28 [32], slip next 15 sts onto a st holder, cast on 3 sts, T1. 32 [36] sts.

Work 9 [11] rounds in patt.

**Shape mitt top

2nd size only

Dec round: (K1, sl1, k1, psso, patt 12, k2tog, k1) twice. 32 sts.

Work 1 round.

For both sizes

Dec round: (K1, sl1, k1, psso, patt 10, k2tog, k1) twice. 28 sts.

Work 1 round.

Dec round: (K1, sl1, k1, psso, patt 8, k2tog, k1) twice. 24 sts.

Work 1 round.

Dec round: (K1, sl1, k1, psso, patt 6, k2tog, k1) twice. 20 sts.

Work 1 round.

Divide rem 20 sts between needles as follows: first 10 sts on one needle and rem 10 sts on second needle. Break off yarn leaving a tail approx. 60cm/23½ in in length.

Carefully turn work inside out – you will need to thread the needles and tail of yarn through the hole at tip of mitten.

Place second needle behind first needle, and with a third needle, cast off using the 3-needle cast off method.

Thumb

Slip 15 sts from st holder back onto three 7mm (US 10½) needles.

With RS facing, rejoin yarn and keeping patt correct, patt 15, using A, pick up and knit 3 sts from cast on sts at palm. 18 sts.

Round 1: Knit.

Round 2: Patt 15, k3.

Round 3: Knit.

For 2nd size only

Rep last 2 rounds once more.

For both sizes

Dec round: *K2tog, rep from * to end. 9 sts.

Dec round: *K2tog, rep from * to last st, k1. 5 sts.

Break off yarn, thread through rem 5 sts, draw up tight and fasten off.

**

Right mitt

Using 6.5mm (US 10) needles and B, cast on 24 [27] sts and join to work in the round.

Purl 2 rounds.

Break off B and join in A.

Inc round: (K3, m1) 8 [9] times. 32 [36] sts.

Round 1: *P2, K2, rep from * to end.

Work this round 11 times more.

Change to 7mm (US 10½) needles and knit 2 rounds.

Cont as folls:-

Round 1: *T1, k3, rep from * to end.

Round 2: Knit to end, ensuring you knit together both strands of thrummed sts.

Round 3: *K2, T1, k1, rep from * to end.

Round 4: As round 2.

Shape thumb

Round 1: T1, m1, k3, m1, *T1, k3, rep from * to end. 34 [38] sts.

Round 2: Knit to end, ensuring you knit together both strands of thrummed sts.

Round 3: K1, m1, k2, T1, k2, m1, *k2, T1, k1, rep from * to end. 36 [40] sts.

Round 4: As round 2.

Round 5: T1, m1, k1, T1, k3, T1, k1, m1, *T1, k3, rep from * to end. 38 [42] sts.

Round 6: As round 2.

Round 7: K1, m1, (T1, k3) twice, T1, m1, *k2, T1, k1, rep from * to end. 40 [44] sts.

Round 8: As round 2.

Round 9: T1, m1, k3, (T1, k3) twice, m1, *T1, k3, rep from * to end. 42 [46] sts.

Round 10: As round 2.

Round 11: K1, m1, k2, (T1, k3) twice, T1, k2, m1, *k2, T1, k1, rep from * to end. 44 [48] sts.

Round 12: As round 2.

Divide for thumb

Next round: T1, cast on 3 sts, slip next 15 sts onto a st holder, patt to end. 32 [36] sts.

Work 9 [11] rounds in patt.

Complete right mitt as given for left mitt from ** to **.

FINISHING

Weave in ends – but not thrummed ends.

On inside of work, cut both ends of thrums to approx. 3cm/1in in length, roll together between fingers to start the felting process (this will continue in wear).

TULLOCH

---

rowan felted tweed

BY RACHEL COOPEY

TULLOCH

BY RACHEL COOPEY

YARN

Rowan Felted Tweed

For hat

A – Duck Egg 173 1 x 50gm

B – Ancient 172 1 x 50gm

For mittens

A – Duck Egg 173 1 x 50gm

B – Ancient 172 1 x 50gm

NEEDLES

3mm (no 11) (US 2/3) 40cm/16in circular needle or dpns for hat only.

3.25mm (no 10) (US 3) 40cm/16in circular needle or dpns.

FINISHED SIZE

Hat – Circumference 56 [60:64]cm/22 [23½:25]in, intended to be worn with 0-5 cm/0-2in positive ease.

Mittens – Circumference 18 [20:22]cm/7 [8:8¾]in, length 25cm/10in

TENSION

30 sts and 36 rounds to 10cm/4in measured over st st colourwork using 3.25mm (US 3) circular needle.

HAT

Using A and 3mm (US 2/3) circular needle cast on 168 [180:198] sts.

Join to work in the round, taking care to ensure sts are not twisted.

Place marker at beg of round.

Rib round: * K1 tbl, p1, rep from * to end.

Using A work the rib round once more.

Change to B and work the rib round 11 times more.

Change to 3.25mm (US 3) needle.

Using the Fair Isle technique work rounds 1-55 as set on chart A. The chart is repeated 28 [30:32] times across the round.

Using A, knit 2 rounds. (Colour B can be cut as the remainder of the hat will be worked using colour A).

Shape crown

Round 1: *K10, k2tog, rep from * to end.

154 [165:176] sts.

Round 2: Knit.

Round 3: *K9, k2tog, rep from * to end.
140 [150:160] sts.

Round 4: Knit.

Round 5: *K8, k2tog, rep from * to end.
126 [135:144] sts.

Round 6: Knit.

Round 7: *K7, k2tog, rep from * to end.
112 [120:128] sts.

Round 8: Knit.

Round 9: *K6, k2tog, rep from * to end.
98 [105:112] sts.

Round 10: Knit.

Round 11: *K5, k2tog, rep from * to end.
84 [90:96] sts.

Round 12: Knit.

Round 13: *K4, k2tog, rep from * to end.
70 [75:80] sts.

Round 14: Knit.

Round 15: *K3, k2tog, rep from * to end.
56 [60:64] sts.

Round 16: Knit.

Round 17: *K2, k2tog, rep from * to end.
42 [45:48] sts.

Round 18: Knit.

Round 19: *K1, k2tog, rep from * to end.
28 [30:32] sts.

Round 20: Knit.

Round 21: *K2tog, rep from * to end.
14 [15:16] sts.

Cut yarn, leaving a 15cm/6in tail, draw the tail through the
rem sts and fasten off.

Weave in ends but do not trim, block to size before trimming
ends.

MITTENS

Using A and 3.25mm (US 3) circular needle cast on 54
[60:66] sts.

Join to work in the round, taking care to ensure sts are
not twisted.

Place marker at beg of round.

Rib round: *K1 tbl, p1, rep from * to end.

Using A work the rib round once more.

Change to B and work the rib round 9 times more.

Using the Fair Isle technique work rounds 1-36 of chart A.

(The chart is repeated 9 [10:11] times across the round.)

Right Mitten: Work round 37 of chart A for 29 [32:35] sts,
k10 on to waste yarn, slip these stitches back on to the left
needle and knit them in pattern, continue in pattern to end
of round.

Left Mitten: Work round 37 of chart A for 15 [18:21] sts,
k10 on to waste yarn, slip these stitches back on to the left
needle and knit them in pattern, continue in pattern to end
of round.

For both mittens

Work rounds 38-55 of chart A.

Using A, knit 10 rounds. (Colour B can be cut as the
remainder of the mittens will be worked using colour A.)

Next round: K27 [30:33], pm, k27 [30:33].

Round 1: K1, ssk, knit to 3 sts before marker, k2tog, k2, ssk,
knit until 3 sts rem, k2tog, k1.

Round 2: Knit.

Rep these 2 rounds until 22 [28:34] sts rem. Cut yarn, leaving
a 46cm/18in tail.

Graft these sts together using Kitchener stitch.

Thumb

Pick up the right leg of the stitches along the bottom of the
waste yarn. Turn the mitten and repeat the process, picking
up the stitches from the other side of the waste yarn. You
should now have 20 stitches on your needles. Remove the
waste yarn.

Using A beg to work in the round as folls:-

K10, pick up 2 stitches in the gap, k10, pick up 2 stitches in
the gap. 24 sts.

Next round: [K10, k2tog] twice. 22 sts.

Knit all stitches until the thumb measures 2cm/¾in less than
the desired length.

Next round: K11, pm, k11.

Cont as folls:-

Round 1: K1, ssk, knit until 3 before marker, k2tog, k2, ssk,
knit until 3 stitches remain, k2tog, k1.

Round 2: Knit.

Rep these 2 rounds until 10 sts rem.

Cut yarn, leaving a 15cm/6in tail.

Graft sts together using Kitchener stitch.

Weave in ends but do not trim, block to size before trimming ends.

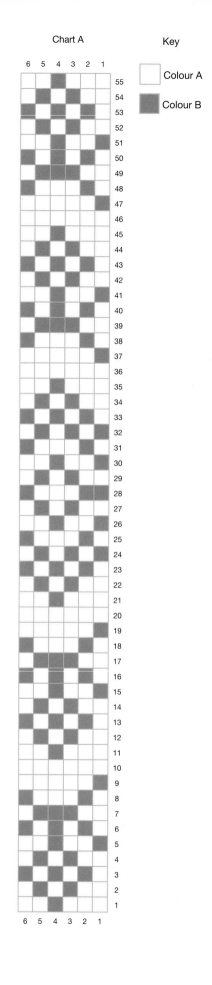

MULCH

rowan fine art

BY RACHEL ATKINSON

MULCH

BY RACHEL ATKINSON

SIZE

S	M	L	
18	20	23	cm
7	8	9	in

Leg length to start of heel: approx. 16cm/6¼in

YARN

Rowan Fine Art

For all sizes 1 x 100gm

(shown in Rowan 314)

NEEDLES

2.25mm (no 13) (US 1) double-pointed needles or
2.25mm (no 13) (US 1) circular needle if working the
magic loop technique.

TENSION

32 sts and 42 rounds to 10cm/4in measured over st st on
2.25mm (US 1) needles

Each 16 row chart rep = 3.5cm /1¼in

SPECIAL ABBREVIATIONS

CDD – slip 2 sts together knitwise, k1, pass 2 slipped
stitches over.

SPECIAL STITCHES

Leaf Cluster Stitch (indicated by the purple cells and
worked over 7 rounds) (see inset for chart)

Round 1: Into 1 stitch work k1, yo, k1, yo, k1. 5 sts.

Rounds 2 – 4: Knit.

Round 5: Ssk, k1, k2tog. 3 sts.

Round 6: Knit.

Round 7: CDD. 1 st.

PATTERN NOTES

The shaded stitch 1 of Medium size Leg B is worked for the leg but not for the instep.
Disregard this stitch from the start of the gusset to the end.

PATTERN BEGINS
CUFF

Cast on 56 (64:72) sts.

Join to work in round, taking care to ensure sts are not twisted.

Place marker at beg of round.

Sizes S and L:

Round 1: * P1, K1tbl, rep from * to end.
Rep round 1 until cuff measures 3cm/1in.

Size M:

Round 1: * K1tbl, p1, rep from * to end.
Rep round 1 until cuff measures 3cm/1in.

LEG
Sizes S and L:

Note: For size S work the sts inside the red border

Round 1: Work Front Leg A chart over first 31 [39] sts, work Back Leg chart over next 25 [33] sts.
This round sets chart placement.
Work 16 rows of patt as set on chart.

Round 17: Work Front Leg B chart over first 31 [39] sts, and cont working Back Leg chart over next 25 [33] sts.

This round sets chart placement.
Work rows 1 – 16 of both charts once, then rows 1 – 7 once more.

Size M:

Round 1: Work as set on Leg A chart twice.
This round sets chart placement.
Work 16 row patt as set on chart twice.
Round 33: Work row 1 of Leg B chart twice.

Work rows 1 – 16 once, then rows 1 – 7 once more.

HEEL FLAP
Sizes S and L: Turn your work so WS is facing. Heel flap will be worked over 25 [33] sts. Rearrange your sts as required leaving 31 [39] sts on hold for instep.

Size M: Work first st of next round, turn your work so WS is facing. Heel flap will be worked over 33 sts. Rearrange your sts as required leaving 31 sts on hold for instep.

All sizes again:

Row 1 (WS): Sl 1 pwise wyif, p24 [32:32].
Row 2 (RS): * Sl 1 pwise wyib, k1, rep from * to last st, k1.
Rep rows 1 and 2 a further 15 times then row 1 once more.

Shape heel (worked in rows)
Row 1 (RS): Sl 1 pwise wyib, k13 [17:17], ssk, k1, turn.
Row 2 (WS): Sl 1 pwise wyif, p4 [4:4], p2tog, p1, turn.
Row 3: Sl 1 pwise wyib, k to 1 st before gap, ssk, k1, turn.
Row 4: Sl 1 pwise wyif, p to 1 st before gap, p2tog, p1, turn.
Rep rows 3 and 4 until all sts have been worked and 15 [19:19] sts rem.

Shape foot gusset
Set-Up Round (RS): Sl 1 kwise wyib, k14 [18:18], pick up and k17 [17:17] sts along the edge of the heel flap, work row 8 of chart across the 31 [31:39] instep sts, pick up and k17 [17:17] sts along the opposite edge of the heel flap, k33 [35:35]. This is new beginning of round.
80 [84:92] sts.

Round 1: Work next row of chart across instep, ssk, k to last 2 sts of round, k2tog. 78 [82:88] sts.

Round 2: Work next row of chart across instep, k to end.
Rep rounds 1 and 2 12 [10:9] times more.
54 [62:70] sts.

Work straight in pattern as set, working chart across instep and knitting the sole sts until foot measures 4 [4:5]cm/1½

[1½:2]in less than desired length ending with either row 8 or 16 of chart.

Shape toe

Round 1: K1, ssk, k to 3 sts before end of instep, k2tog, k2, ssk, k to 3 sts before end of sole, k2tog, k1. 50 [58:66] sts.

Round 2: Knit.

Rep rounds 1 and 2 until 22 [26:26] sts rem.

Break yarn leaving a 30cm/12in tail.

Graft sts together using Kitchener stitch.

Weave in ends and block.

LEG A - MEDIUM

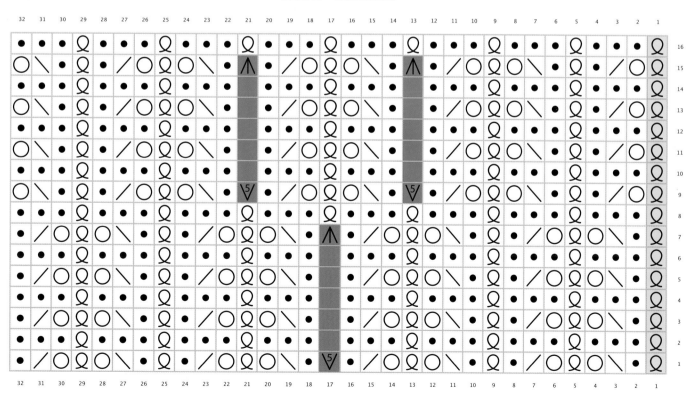

LEG B - MEDIUM

FRONT LEG A - SMALL/LARGE

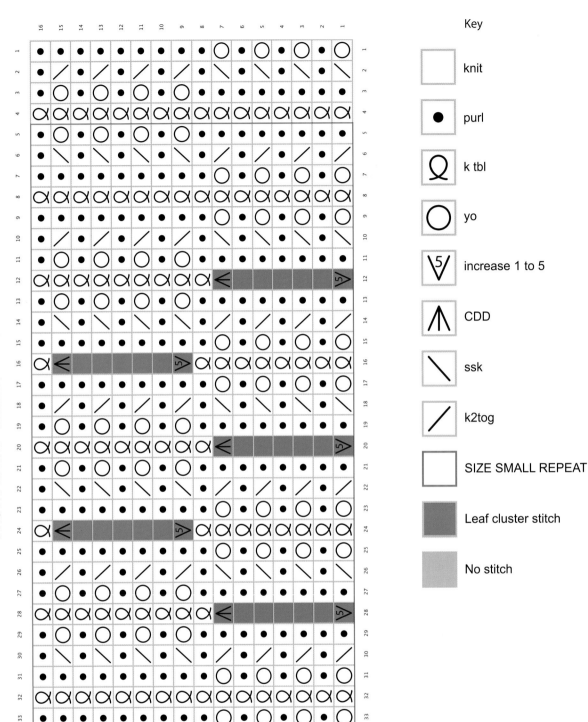

Key

knit

● purl

Ϙ k tbl

◯ yo

\|5/ increase 1 to 5

⋀ CDD

\ ssk

/ k2tog

SIZE SMALL REPEAT

Leaf cluster stitch

No stitch

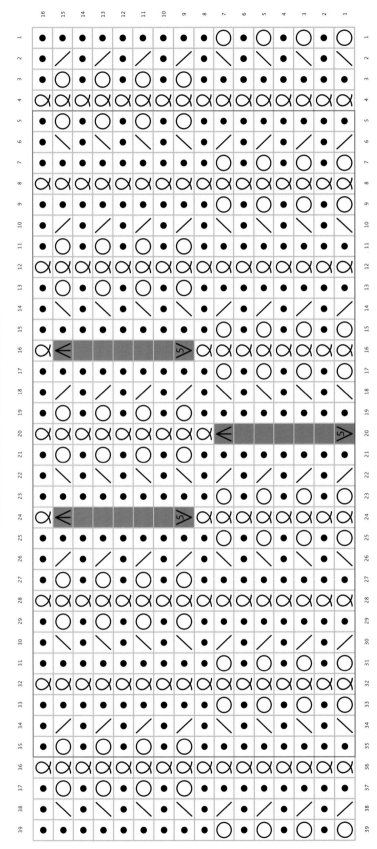

LEAF CLUSTER STITCH

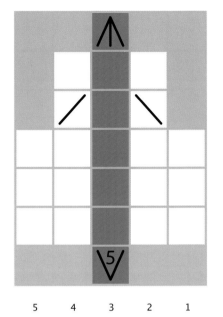

YEW

rowan big wool

BY ANDI SATTERLUND

YEW

BY ANDI SATTERLUND

YARN

Rowan Big Wool

3 x 100gm

(shown in Smoky 007)

FINISHED SIZE

170cm/67in in circumference

NEEDLES

10mm (no 000) (US 15) circular needle

TENSION

8 sts and 13 rounds to 10cm/4in measured over pattern using 10mm (US 15) needles.

LOOP SCARF

Cast on 135 sts.

Join to work in round, taking care to ensure sts are not twisted.

Place marker at beg of round.

Round 1 and all foll alt rounds: * (P1, k1) 3 times, p1, k7, p1, rep from * to end.

Round 2: * (K1, p1) 3 times, p1, (k1, yo) twice, sk2po, k2, p1, rep from * to end.

Round 4: * (K1, p1) 3 times, p1, k1, yo, k3, yo, sk2po, p1, rep from * to end.

Round 6 and 8: * (K1, p1) 3 times, p1, k1, yo, ssk, k1, k2tog, yo, k1, p1, rep from * to end.

Round 10: * (K1, p1) 3 times, p1, k2, k3tog, (yo, k1) twice, p1, rep from * to end.

Round 12: * (K1, p1) 3 times, p1, k3tog, yo, k3, yo, k1, p1, rep from * to end.

Rounds 14 and 16: Rep rounds 6 and 8.

Rounds 17 to 28: Rep rounds 1-12.

Cast off in pattern.

FINISHING

Weave in all ends. Press/block as described on the information page.

HAWTHORN

rowan pure wool dk

BY ANDI SATTERLUND

HAWTHORN

BY ANDI SATTERLUND

TENSION

24 sts and 30 rounds to 10cm/4in measured over st st and Fair Isle using 3.75mm (US 5) needles.

HAT

Using A cast on 120 sts.

Join to work in round, taking care to ensure sts are not twisted.

Place marker at beg of round.

Round 1: * K1, p1, rep from * to end.

This round sets rib.

Work 9 rows more in rib.

Rounds 11 and 12: Using yarn A, knit.

Rounds 13 to 17: Work as given on Chart A.

Rounds 18 to 30: Using yarn B, knit.

Rounds 31 to 38: Work as given on Chart B.

Rounds 39 to 46: Using yarn A, knit.

Round 47: Using yarn A, (ssk, k16, k2tog) 6 times. 108 sts.

Round 48: Work in st st with yarn A.

Shape crown

Using yarn A throughout cont as folls:-

Round 49: (Ssk, k14, k2tog) 6 times. 96 sts.

Round 50: Knit.

Round 51: (Ssk, k12, k2tog) 6 times. 84 sts.

Round 52: Knit.

Continue to decrease as set until 12 sts rem.

Next round: K2tog to end. 6 sts.

Break yarn and thread through remaining stitches.
Fasten off.

FINISHING

Weave in ends but do not trim. Make pompon approx.
8cm/3in in diameter, using leftover yarn. Block hat to size
and secure pompon on top of crown. Trim ends.

CHART A

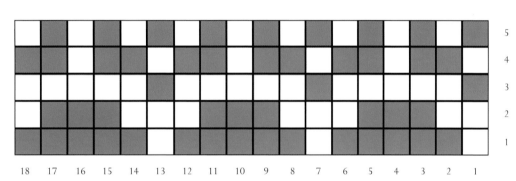

CHART B

KEY

 YARN A

☐ YARN B

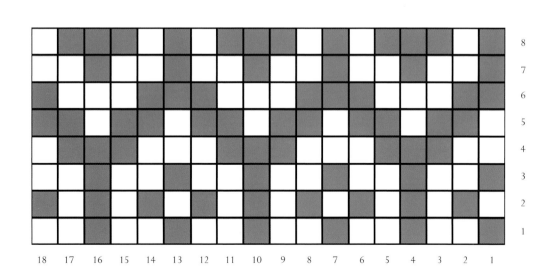

HAWTHORN WRISTWARMERS

YARN

Rowan Pure Wool DK

A – Port 037 1 x 50gm

B – Anthracite 003 1 x 50gm

FINISHED SIZE

Knuckle circumference: 18 [20:23]cm/7 [8:9]in

NEEDLES

1 set 3.75mm (no 9) (US 5) dpns or 3.75mm (no 9) (US 5) circular needle if working the magic loop technique.

TENSION

24 sts and 30 rounds to 10cm/4in measured over st st and Fair Isle using 3.75mm (US 5) needles.

WRISTWARMER (Make 2)

Cuff

Using yarn A cast on 42 [48:54] sts.

Join to work in round, taking care to ensure sts are not twisted.

Place marker at beg of round.

Round 1: * K1, p1, rep from * to end.

This round sets rib.

Work 9 rounds more in rib.

Rounds 11 and 12: Using yarn A, knit.

Rounds 13 to 17: Work as given on Chart A.

Gusset shaping

Using yarn B throughout, knit 0 (2:4) rounds.

Next Round: K1, pm, k2, pm, knit to end.

Next Round: Knit to marker, sm, m1, knit to marker, m1, sm, knit to end. 44 [50:56] sts.

Next Round: Knit.

Rep the last two rounds 4 (5:6) times more.

52 [60:68] sts.

Knit 2 rounds.

Remove gusset markers.

Shaping knuckles

Next Round: K1, place next 12 (14:16) sts on holder, cast on 2 sts, knit to end. 42 [48:54] sts.

Next 8 Rounds: Work as given on Chart B.

Next Round: Using yarn A, knit.

Next 5 Rounds: Using yarn A work 5 rounds in 1x1 rib. Cast off in rib.

Thumb

Using yarn B throughout, cont as folls:-

Round 1: Starting at the centre of the cast on 2 sts, using yarn B, pick up and knit 2, knit across 12 [14:16] sts from holder, pick up and knit 2, pm and join in the round. 16 [18:20] sts.

Round 2: K0 (0:1), k2tog, knit to last 2 [2:3] sts, ssk, k0 [0:1]. 14 [16:18] sts.

Round 3: Knit.

Rounds 4 to 7: Work in rib as set.

Cast off in rib.

FINISHING

Weave in ends and block.

BUD

rowan big wool

BY GEMMA ATKINSON

BUD

BY GEMMA ATKINSON

YARN

Big Wool

3 x 100gm   (shown in Reseda 069)

NEEDLES

9mm (no 00) (US 13) circular needle
80cm/32in long

10mm (no 000) (US 15) circular needles
80cm/32in long

Cable needle

TENSION

9.5 sts and 12 rows to 10cm/4in measured over rib
(when slightly stretched) on 10mm (US 15) needles.

Cable panel of 16 sts measures 13cm/5in.

FINISHED SIZE

Completed cowl measures 32cm/12½in in depth and has
a circumference of approx. 91cm/36in across
cabled section.

SPECIAL ABBREVIATIONS

C4F = slip next 2 sts onto cable needle and leave at front
of work, K2, then K2 from cable needle.

C4B = slip next 2 sts onto cable needle and leave at back
of work, K2, then K2 from cable needle.

C6F = slip next 3 sts onto cable needle and leave at front
of work, K3, then K3 from cable needle.

C6B = slip next 3 sts onto cable needle and leave at back
of work, K3, then K3 from cable needle.

COWL

Using 10mm (US 15) circular needles, cast on 112 sts.
Join to work in round, taking care to ensure sts are
not twisted.
Place marker at beg of round.
Round 1: *K2, P2, rep from * to end
This round forms rib.
Cont in rib for a further 11 rows.
Round 13: * P3, k4, p3, k6, rep from * to end.
Rounds 14 and 15: As round 13.

Round 16: * P3, C4F, p3, C6F, p3, C4B, p3, C6F, rep from * to last 16 sts, p3, C4F, p3, C6F.

Rounds 17 – 19: As rounds 13-15.

Round 20: * P3, C4F, p3, C6B, p3, C4B, p3, C6B, rep from * to last 16 sts, p3, C4F, p3, C6B.

These last 8 rounds form patt.

Cont in patt for a further 7 rounds.

Next round: P1, p2tog, *C4F, p1, p2tog, C6B, P3, C4B, P1, P2tog, C6B, P3, rep from * to last 13 sts, C4F, p1, p2tog, C6B. 104 sts.

Change to 9mm (US 13) circular needles.

Next round: *P2, K2, rep from * to end.

This round forms rib.

Cont in rib for a further 9 rows.

Next round: *P2tog, K2tog, rep from * to end. 52 sts.

Cast off in rib.

FINISHING

Press/block as described on the information page.

Sew in any loose ends.

LEIGH

rowan fine art

BY SARA THORNETT

LEIGH

BY SARA THORNETT

SIZES - Foot circumference

S	M	L
20	23	25 cm
8	9	10 in

Leg length to start of heel 14cm/5½in

YARN

Rowan Fine Art

For all sizes 2 x 100gm
(shown in Lapwing 306)

NEEDLES

Set of 4 double-pointed 2.5mm (no 12) (US 2) needles
(dpns) or circular needle if using the magic loop technique

Cable needle

TENSION

50 sts and 50 rows to 10cm/4in measured over patt using
2.5mm (US 2) needles.

SPECIAL ABBREVIATIONS

C10Bw – slip the next 5 stitches onto cable needle and
leave at back of work, K5, then K5 from cable needle.

N – needle

Wrap stitch – take the yarn through the needles to the
other side of the work, slip the next stitch (purlwise),
take the yarn back through the needles, return the slipped
stitch to the left needle, turn. When working over the
wrapped stitches ensure to pick up the wrapped bar as
well as the relevant stitch.

SOCKS (both alike)
Using Thumb method, cast on 120 [130:140] sts.
Turn and knit onto separate dpns as folls: K40 [40:50]
onto N1, K40 [50:40] onto N2, K40 [40:50] onto N3.
Join to work in round, taking care to ensure sts are not
twisted.

Place marker at beg of round.

Rounds 1 to 7: Knit.

Round 8: * C10Bw, rep from * to end.

Rounds 9 to 17: Knit.

Rep rounds 8 to 17 5 times more.

Next round: Work as given for round 8.

Next 3 rounds: Knit.

Decrease round: *K1, k2tog, rep from * to last 0 [1:2] sts, k0 [1:2]. 80 [87:94] sts.

Next round: Knit.

Shape heel (to be worked in rows)

Next row: K17 [18:19], wrap next st, turn.

Next row: P34 [36:38], wrap next st, turn.

Next row: K33 [35:37] ,wrap next st, turn.

Cont in this way, working 1 st less on each row until the following row has been completed – P16, wrap next st, turn.

For all sizes

Next row: K17 – wrap next st, turn.

Next row: P18 – wrap next st, turn.

Cont in this way, working 1 st more on each row until the following row has been completed – P36 [40:40], wrap next st, turn.

All sizes

Knit to marker at start of round.

Shape foot gusset

Next round: K19 [20:21], k2tog, k38 [41:48], k2togtbl, k19 [20:21]. 78 [85:92] sts.

Next round: Knit.

Next round: K19 [20:21], K2tog, K36 [39:46], k2togtbl, k19 (20:21). 76 [83: 90] sts.

Next round: Knit.

The last 2 rounds set decreases.

Dec as set until the following round has been worked – K19 [20:21], k2tog, k28 (29:32), k2togtbl, k19 [20:21]. 68 [73:76] sts.

Size M only

Next round: K36, K2tog, K35. 72 sts.

For all sizes

Redistribute the stitches on the needles as follows: 22 [23:25] sts on N1, 24 [23:26] sts on N2 and 22 [23:25] sts on N3.

Cont to knit in rounds until foot measures 19.5 [22:23.5]cm/7½ [8½:9]in, or 3 [3:3.5]cm/1 [1:1¼]in less than the desired foot length.

Shape toe

Next round: Knit.

Next round: K15 [16:17], k2tog, k2togtbl, k30 [32:34], k2tog, k2togtbl, k15 [16:17].

These 2 rows set toe decreases.

Dec as set until the following round has been completed – K10[11:12], k2tog, k2togtbl, k20 [22:24], k2tog, k2togtbl, k10 [11:12].

For sizes M and L only

Next round: K[10:11], k2tog, k2togtbl, k[20:22], k2tog, k2togtbl, k[10:11].

For size L only

Next round: Knit.

Next round: K10, k2tog, k2togtbl, k20, k2tog, k2togtbl, k10.

For all sizes

Next round: K9, k2tog, k2togtbl, k18, k2tog, k2togtbl, k9.

Next round: K8, k2tog, k2togtbl, k16, k2tog, k2togtbl, k8.

Next round: K7, k2tog, k2togtbl, k14, k2tog, k2togtbl, k7.

Knit 8 sts.

Slip sts on N1 onto N3 – the stitches are now split between 2 needles (16 sts on each)

Graft sts together using Kitchener stitch.

Weave in ends.

HOUNDSTOOTH

rowan kidsilk haze

BY GEMMA ATKINSON

HOUNDSTOOTH

BY GEMMA ATKINSON

YARN

Kidsilk Haze

A Blackcurrant 641   1 x 25gm

B Ultra 659   1 x 25gm

NEEDLES

1 pair 4mm (no 8) (US 6) needles

FINISHED SIZE

Completed headband measures 7 cm/2¾in in width
when folded and has a circumference of 50 cm/19½in.

TENSION

28 sts and 23 rows to 10cm/4in measured over patterned
st st using 4mm (US 6) needles and yarn held **DOUBLE**.

Using 4mm (US 6) needles and yarn A held **DOUBLE**,
cast on 40 sts.

Row 1 (RS): K1A, *k1B, k3A, rep from * to last 3 sts,
k1B, k2A.
Row 2: * P3B, P1A, rep from * to end.
Row 3: * K3B, k1A, rep from * to end.
Row 4: P1A, * p1B, p3A, rep from * to last 3 sts, p1B,
p2A.

These 4 rows form patt.

Cont in patt until work measures 50cm/19½in, ending
after row 4 of patt and with RS facing for next row.

Cast off.

FINISHING

Press/block as described on page 102.

Sew in any loose ends.

Centre band

Using 4mm (US 6) needles and yarn B **DOUBLE**, cast on 12 sts.

Work in g st until work measures 6cm/2½in, ending with RS facing for next row.

Cast off.

FINISHING

Join row end edges together of headband using mattress stitch, and then sew together both open ends of headband.

Join both cast on and cast off edges together and attach centre band over the join, sewing together cast on and cast off edge of centre band.

FOXGLOVE

---

rowan pure wool dk

BY SARA THORNETT

FOXGLOVE

BY SARA THORNETT

YARN

Rowan Pure Wool Dk

Hat: 2 x 50gm

Hand Warmers: 2 x 50gm

(both shown in Damson 030)

NEEDLES

1 pair 3.25mm (no 10) (US 3) needles

1 pair 4.5mm (no 7) (US 7) needles

1 set of 3.25mm (no 10) (US 3) dpns or 3.25mm (no 10) (US 3) circular needle if using the magic loop technique, for handwarmers.

Stitch holders for handwarmers.

FINSHED SIZE

To fit an average adult head/hand.

TENSION

32 sts and 16 rows to 10cm/4in measured over patt using 4.5mm (US 7) needles.

HAT

Using 3.25mm (US 3) needles, cast on 126 sts.

Row 1 (RS): K2, * p2, k2, rep from * to end.

Row 2: * P2, k2, rep from * to last 2 sts, p2.

These 2 rows form rib.

Work in rib for a further 10 rows, ending with RS facing for next row.

Row 13: Knit.

Change to 4.5mm (US 7) needles.

Work patt as follows:

Row 1 (WS): K1, P to last st, wrapping the yarn around the needle twice for each st, K1.

Row 2: K1, * sl the next 4 sts from left needle to right (purlwise) dropping the extra yarn wrap, return these 4 sts to the left needle (purlwise), work these 4 sts together working k1, p1, k1, p1 into these sts, rep from * to last st, k1.

Row 3: K1, p2, P to last 3 sts, wrapping the yarn around the needle twice for each st, p2, k1.

Row 4: K3, * sl the next 4 sts from left needle to right (purlwise) dropping the extra yarn wrap, return these 4 sts to the left needle (purlwise), work these 4 sts together working k1, p1, k1, p1 into these sts, rep from * to last 3 sts, k3.

These 4 rows for[m patt.]

Continue in patt u[ntil me]asures 18.5cm/7¼in, ending with row 4 of patt[.]

Shape crown

Row 1 (WS, row [decrease]**):** K1, * patt 4 sts, k1, p2, k1, rep from * to last [5 st]s, k1.

Row 2: K1, * patt 4 sts, k1, p2tog, k1, rep from * to last 5 sts, patt 4 sts, k1. 111 sts.

Row 3: K1, * p1, k2, p1, k1, p1, k1, rep from * to last 5 sts, p1, k2, p1, k1.

Row 4: K1, p1, * K2tog, p1, k1, p1, k1, p1, rep from * to last 4 sts, k2tog, p1, k1. 95 sts.

Row 5: K1, * p1, k1, rep from * to end.

Row 6: Work as given for row 5.

Row 7: K1, * p1, k1, p1, k3tog, rep from * to last 4 sts, (p1, k1) twice. 65 sts.

Row 8: Work as given for row 5.

Row 9: Work as given for row 5.

Row 10: K1, p1, k1, * p3tog, k1, rep from * to last 2 sts, p1, k1. 35 sts.

Row 11: Work as given for row 5.

Row 12: K1, p1, * k3tog, p1, rep from * to last st, k1. 19 sts.

Break yarn and thread through rem sts. Pull up tight and fasten off.

FINISHING

Join back seam. Weave in ends but do not trim. Press/block hat to size. Trim ends.

HANDWARMERS (both alike)

Using 3.25mm (US 3) needles cast on 58 sts.
Row 1 (RS): K2, * p2, k2, rep from * to end.
Row 2: * P2, k2, rep from * to last 2 sts, p2.
These 2 rows form rib.
Work in rib for a further 24 rows, ending with RS facing for next row.
Row 27: Knit.
Change to 4.5mm (US 7) needles.
Row 1 (WS): K1, P to last st, wrapping the yarn around the needle twice for each st, k1.
Row 2: K1, * sl the next 4 sts from left needle to right (purlwise) dropping the extra yarn wrap, return these 4 sts to the left needle (purlwise), working these 4 sts together working k1, p1, k1, p1 into these sts, rep from * to last st, k1.
Row 3: K1, p2, p to last 3 sts, wrapping the yarn around the needle twice for each st, p2, k1.
Row 4: K3, * sl the next 4 sts from left needle to right

(purlwise) dropping the extra yarn wrap, return these 4 sts to the left needle (purlwise), working these 4 sts together working k1, p1, k1, p1 into these sts, rep from * to last 3 sts, k3.
These 4 rows form patt.
Work 5 rows more as set.

Split for thumb

Keeping patt correct, cont as folls:-
Next row (RS): Patt 29, turn, leaving rem sts on a holder.
Next row: Cast on 1 st at beg of row (this is in place of the K1 of the patt row), patt to end.
Work 9 rows more in patt.
Break yarn and leave sts on a 2nd holder.
Return to sts on 1st holder, rejoin yarn with RS facing.
Next row (RS): Cast on 1 st at beg of row (this is in place of the K1 of the patt row), patt to end.
Work 10 rows more in patt, ending with **WS** facing for next row.

Join sections

Next row (WS): Patt 28, (work the next 2 sts tog in patt) twice, patt to end.
Work 5 rows more in patt.
Next row (WS): Purl.
Change to 3.25mm (US 3) needles.
Work 10 rows in rib as set.
Cast off in rib.

Thumb

With RS facing and using 3.25mm (US 3) dpns, begin at top of thumb opening, pick up and knit 24 sts evenly around the opening (distributing these sts evenly on 3 of the dpns)
Round 1 (RS): * K2, p2, rep from * to end.
This round forms rib.
Work 9 rounds more in rib.
Cast off in rib.

FINISHING

Join side seam. Weave in ends and press/block handwarmers.

TECHNIQUES

MAGIC LOOP TECHNIQUE

The magic loop technique is a really useful technique for working in the round when you have a smaller circumference than would fit all the way around a circular needle.

It's also great for people who have avoided socks as they involve double-pointed needles, which can be terrifying!

1: Once you have cast on the desired number of stitches and you are ready to start working in the round, divide your sts roughly in two. Pull your wire through the middle of these two sets of stitches.

2: With the set of stitches with the yarn attached left on the middle of the wire, the remaining stitches will be pushed on to the needle nearest to them. By holding the stitches in this position those on the wire and those on the needle sit right next to each other and this will stop a ladder from forming in your work.

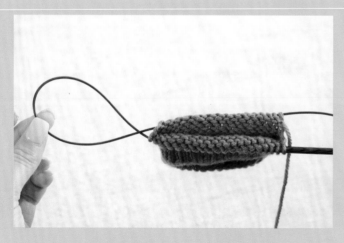

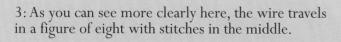

3: As you can see more clearly here, the wire travels in a figure of eight with stitches in the middle.

4: Once you have worked across the stitches on the needle, it is time to change the wire position, so turn your work.

5: As the stitches just worked now have the yarn attached to them they belong on the wire and the set on the wire needs to be shuffled onto the needle nearest them.

6: Now that the position of the stitches has changed you can work across the second half of the stitches.

KITCHENER STITCH

This technique gives a neat, seamless edge to the toes of the sock designs in the book.

1: Divide the sts evenly between two needles and hold them parallel to each other. The wrong sides of the work should be facing each other and the tips of the needles you are to work from should face in the same direction.

2: Thread a tapestry needle with the tail end of the yarn.

3: Take the needle through the first stitch on the front needle from back to front of work as shown (as if purling).

4: Take the needle through the first stitch on the back needle from front to back of work (as if knitting).

5: Take the needle through the first stitch on the front needle from the front (as if knitting) and slip this stitch off the knitting needle.

6: Take needle through the next stitch on the front needle from the back (as if purling). Leave this stitch on the needle.

7: Take needle through the first stitch on the back needle from the back (as if purling). This stitch can now be slipped off the knitting needle.

8: Take needle through the next stitch on the back needle from the front (as if knitting). Leave this stitch on the needle.

Steps 4 to 8 will now be repeated until all stitches have been worked.

TIP: We would suggest working the Kitchener stitch loosely and then using the tip of the sewing needle to work across the row, tightening up the stitches until they are neat.

INFORMATION

TENSION

Obtaining the correct tension is perhaps the single factor which can make the greatest difference to your finished project. The different designers featured in this book have each set their own tension for each project and this is given at the beginning of each pattern.

We recommend that you knit a square in the pattern suggested of approx. 5 stitches and 6 rows more than given in the tension notes. Mark out the centre 10cm/4in and count the number of stitches and rows in this section. If there are more stitches to 10cm you may need to change to a bigger needle and if there are less you should try a smaller needle.

Once you have achieved the correct tension you are ready to start knitting your project.

CHART NOTES

Each square on a chart represents a stitch of your knitting.

When working back and forth in rows from the charts, read odd rows (usually knit) from right to left and even rows (usually purl) from left to right. When working in the round, read all rows from right to left.

FAIR ISLE KNITTING

When working two or more colours across a row, strand the yarn not in use loosely across the back of your work. If this yarn travels across more than 3 or 4 stitches we recommend taking it under and over the colour in use to catch it in place.

BLOCKING/PRESSING

We recommend, unless otherwise stated in the pattern, to lightly press the project by covering it with damp cloths and leaving until dry.

For those projects that recommend blocking you sew in the ends but do not trim them. Soak the shawl in tepid water for 20 mins. Squeeze gently to remove excess water; you may wish to roll your project in a towel to remove more water. Pin the project out to the measurements given and leave until dry. Once dry trim yarn ends.

ABBREVIATIONS

alt – alternate

beg – begin(ning)

cm – centimetres

cont – continue

dec – decreas(e)(ing)

dpn – double-pointed needle

foll – following

g st – garter stitch (every row knit)

gm – grams

in – inch(es)

inc – increas(e)(ing)

K – knit

meas – measures

mm – millimetres

m1 – make one stitch by picking up loop between last and next stitch and working into the back of this loop

P – purl

patt – pattern

pm – place marker

psso – pass slipped stitch over

p2sso – pass 2 slipped stitches over

rem – remain(ing)

RS – right side

sk2po – slip 1 stitch knitwise, knit 2 stitches together, pass slipped stitch over

sl 1 – slip one stitch

sm – slip marker

ssk – slip 2 stitches knitwise one at a time, knit the two slipped stitches together through the back of the loops

st(s) – stitch(es)

st st – stocking stitch (1 row knit, 1 row purl)

tbl – through back of loop

tog – together

WS – wrong side

wyib – with yarn in back

wyif – with yarn in front

yo – yarn over

0 – no stitches, times or rows

Stockists

AUSTRALIA: Australian Country Spinners, Pty Ltd, Level 7, 409 St. Kilda Road, Melbourne Vic 3004. Tel: 03 9380 3888 Fax: 03 9820 0989 Email: customerservice@auspinners.com.au

AUSTRIA: : MEZ Harlander GmbH, Schulhof 6, 1. Stock, 1010 Wien, Austria Tel: + 00800 26 27 28 00 Fax: (00) 49 7644 802-133 Email: verkauf. harlander@mezcrafts.com Web: www.mezcrafts.at

BELGIUM: MEZ crafts Belgium NV, c/o MEZ GmbH, Kaiserstr.1, 79341 Kenzingen Germany Tel: 0032 (0) 800 77 89 2 Fax: 00 49 7644 802 133 Email: sales.be-nl@mezcrafts.com Web: www.mezcrafts.be

BULGARIA: MEZ Crafts Bulgaria EOOD, Bul. Rozhen 25A, BG-1220 Sofia, Bulgaria Tel: +359 2 439 24 24 Fax: +359 2 439 24 28 Email: office.bg@mezcrafts.com

CHINA: Commercial agent Mr Victor Li, c/o MEZ GmbH Germany, Kaiserstr. 1, 79341 Kenzingen / Germany Tel: (86- 21) 13816681825 Email: victor.li@mezcrafts.com

CHINA: SHANGHAI YUJUN CO.,LTD., Room 701 Wangjiao Plaza, No.175 Yan'an(E), 200002 Shanghai, China Tel: +86 2163739785 Email: jessechang@vip.163.com

CYPRUS: MEZ Crafts Bulgaria EOOD, Bul. Rozhen 25A, BG-1220 Sofia, Bulgaria Tel: +359 2 439 24 24 Fax: +359 2 439 24 28 Email: office.bg@mezcrafts.com

CZECH REPUBLIC: Coats Czecho s.r.o.Staré Mesto 246 569 32 Tel: (420) 461616633 Email: galanterie@coats.com

DENMARK: Carl J. Permin A/S Egegaardsvej 28 DK-2610 Rødovre Tel: (45) 36 72 12 00 E-mail: permin@permin.dk

ESTONIA: MEZ Crafts Estonia OÜ, Ampri tee 9/4, 74001 Viimsi Harjumaa Tel: +372 630 6252 Email: info.ee@mezcrafts.com Web: www.coatscrafts.co.ee

FINLAND: MEZ Crafts Finland Oy, Huhtimontie 6, 04200 Kerava Tel: (358) 9 274 871 Email: sales.fi@mezcrafts.com www.coatscrafts.fi

FRANCE: 3bcom, 35 avenue de Larrieu, 31094 Toulouse cedex 01, France Tel: 0033 (0) 562 202 096 Email: Commercial@3b-com.com

GERMANY: MEZ GmbH, Kaiserstr. 1, 79341 Kenzingen, Germany Tel: 0049 7644 802 222 Email: kenzingen.vertrieb@mezcrafts.com Fax: 0049 7644 802 300 Web: www.mezcrafts.de

GREECE: MEZ Crafts Bulgaria EOOD, Bul. Rozhen 25A, BG-1220 Sofia, Bulgaria Tel: +359 2 439 24 24 Fax: +359 2 439 24 28 Email: office.bg@mezcrafts.com

HOLLAND: G. Brouwer & Zn B.V., Oudhuijzerweg 69, 3648 AB Wilnis, Netherlands Tel: 0031 (0) 297-281 557 Email: info@gbrouwer.nl

HONG KONG: East Unity Company Ltd, Unit B2, 7/F., Block B, Kailey Industrial Centre, 12 Fung Yip Street, Chai Wan Tel: (852)2869 7110 Email: eastunityco@yahoo.com.hk

ICELAND: Carl J. Permin A/S Egegaardsvej 28 DK-2610 Rødovre Tel: (45) 36 72 12 00 Email: permin@permin.dk

ITALY: Mez Cucirini Italy Srl, Viale Sarca, 223, 20126 MILANO Tel.: 02 636151 Fax: 02 66111701

JAPAN: Hobbyra Hobbyre Corporation, 23-37, 5-Chome, Higashi-Ohi, Shinagawa-Ku, 1400011 Tokyo. Tel +81334721104 Daidoh International, 3-8-11 Kudanminami Chiyodaku, Hiei Kudan Bldg 5F, 1018619 Tokyo. Tel +81-3-3222-7076 Fax +81-3-3222-7066

KOREA: My Knit Studio, 3F, 144 Gwanhun-Dong, 110-300 Jongno-Gu, Seoul Tel: 82-2-722-0006 Email: myknit@myknit.com Web: www.myknit.com

LATVIA: Coats Latvija SIA, Mukusalas str. 41 b, Riga LV-1004 Tel: +371 67 625173   Fax: +371 67 892758 Email: info.latvia@coats.com Web: www.coatscrafts.lv

LEBANON: y.knot, Saifi Village, Mkhalissiya Street 162, Beirut Tel: (961) 1 992211 Fax: (961) 1 315553 Email: y.knot@cyberia.net.lb

LITHUANIA & RUSSIA: MEZ Crafts Lithuania UAB, A. Juozapaviciaus str. 6/2, LT-09310 Vilnius Tel: +370 527 30971   Fax: +370 527 2305 Email: info.lt@ mezcrafts.com Web: www.coatscrafts.lt

LUXEMBOURG: Coats N.V., c/o Coats GmbH, Kaiserstr.1, 79341 Kenzingen, Germany Tel: 00 49 7644 802 222   Fax: 00 49 7644 802 133 Email: sales.coatsninove@coats.com Web: www.coatscrafts.be

MEXICO: Estambres Crochet SA de CV, Aaron Saenz 1891-7Pte, 64650 MONTERREY TEL +52 (81) 8335-3870 Email: abremer@redmundial.com.mx

NEW ZEALAND: ACS New Zealand, P.O Box 76199, Northwood, Christchurch, New Zealand Tel: 64 3 323 6665   Fax: 64 3 323 6660 Email: lynn@impactmg.co.nz

NORWAY: Carl J. Permin A/S Egegaardsvej 28 DK-2610 Rødovre Tel: (45) 36 72 12 00   E-mail: permin@permin.dk

PORTUGAL: Mez Crafts Portugal, Lda – Av. Vasco da Gama, 774 - 4431-059 V.N, Gaia, Portugal Tel: 00 351 223 770700 Email: sales.iberia@mezcrafts.com

SINGAPORE: Golden Dragon Store, BLK 203 Henderson Rd #07-02, 159546 Henderson Indurstrial Park Singapore Tel: (65) 62753517   Fax: (65) 62767112   Email: gdscraft@hotmail.com

SLOVAKIA: MEZ Crafts Slovakia, s.r.o. Seberíniho 1, 821 03 Bratislava, Slovakia Tel: +421 2 32 30 31 19   Email: galanteria@mezcrafts.com

SOUTH AFRICA: Arthur Bales LTD, 62 4th Avenue, Linden 2195 Tel: (27) 11 888 2401 Fax: (27) 11 782 6137   Email: arthurb@new.co.za Web: www.arthurbales.co.za

SPAIN: MEZ Fabra Spain S.A, Avda Meridiana 350, pta 13 D, 08027 Barcelona Tel: +34 932908400 Fax: +34 932908409 Email: atencion. clientes@mezcrafts.com

SWEDEN: Carl J. Permin A/S Egegaardsvej 28 DK-2610 Rødovre Tel: (45) 36 72 12 00   E-mail: permin@permin.dk

SWITZERLAND: MEZ Crafts Switzerland GmbH, Stroppelstrasse20, 5417 Untersiggenthal, Switzerland Tel: +41 00800 2627 2800 Fax: 0049 7644 802 133 Email: verkauf.ch@mezcrafts.com Web: www.mezcrafts.ch

TURKEY: MEZ Crafts Tekstil A.Ş, Kavacık Mahallesi, Ekinciler Cad. Necip Fazıl Sok. No.8 Kat: 5, 34810 Beykoz / Istanbul Tel: +90 216 425 88 10   www.mezcrafts.com

TAIWAN: Cactus Quality Co Ltd, 7FL-2, No. 140, Sec.2 Roosevelt Rd, Taipei, 10084 Taiwan, R.O.C. Tel: 00886-2-23656527 Fax: 886-2-23656503 Email: cqcl@ms17.hinet.net

THAILAND: Global Wide Trading, 10 Lad Prao Soi 88, Bangkok 10310 Tel: 00 662 933 9019 Fax: 00 662 933 9110 Email: global.wide@yahoo.com

U.K: Mez Craft UK Ltd, 17F Brooke's Mill, Armitage Bridge Huddersfield, HD4 7NR Tel: +44 (0) 1484 768878   Fax: +44 (0) 1484 690 838 Web: www.knitrowan.com

U.S.A.: Westminster Fibers, 8 Shelter Drive, Greer, South Carolina, 29650 Tel: (800) 445-9276 Fax: 864-879-9432 Email: info@westminsterfibers.com

ACKNOWLEDGEMENTS

First and foremost I would like to thank the incredibly talented designers who agreed to feature in this book.

Thanks also to Kate, David and all the team at Rowan for their constant support.

India, Magnus, Sarah-Alyce, Lauren and Rosie for making the shoot fun despite the rain and doing such a great job.

Last but not least thanks to Jill for checking all the patterns.

– Sarah

PUBLISHER'S ACKNOWLEDGEMENTS

The publisher would like to thank: India Hobson for producing the beautiful photographs. Sarah Hatton for her dedication to the project and for all of her help in bringing the title together.

Kate Buller, David MacLeod and the team at Rowan for believing in the title and supporting the project from the beginning.

Finally the wonderful designers who have been commissioned for this title. We were delighted with all of the submissions we had and think the selected designs all work great together. Thank you.

Follow us at:
www.quailpublishing.co.uk
Twitter: @quail_studio
Instagram: @quail_Studio